SWIMMING THE DREAM

Contents

Written by Ellie Simmonds

Collins

Swimming from the start

I'm the youngest of five. I have three older sisters and one older brother, so it's quite a big family. By the time I was born in 1994, most of my **siblings** had left home, so it was mainly just me and one sister, Katie, plus my mum and dad at home when I was growing up.

I grew up in Sutton Coldfield, in Birmingham, in a large road called Wood Lane. I remember the house really well because of the swimming pool in the back garden, which had a wave machine and was brilliant fun.

on my bike in the back garden

There were two girls across the road – one was the same age as me and the other was the same age as my sister. We all played together – either they'd both come to our house or we'd go to theirs.

It was good that we had the swimming pool because we spent most of our time in it, or we played in the garden. We were always outdoors and on the go, so that's probably why I'm quite an outdoors, active person – I always want to be on the move. From the moment I could talk I'd be asking my mum what we'd be doing that day – I didn't do sitting quietly on my own very well!

I enjoyed most sports, but I really wanted to learn how to swim, so that I could swim in our pool with everyone else. So, just before I was five years old I started swimming lessons, and it went from there. I can never decide what came first, whether swimming suits me because it's a time-consuming sport and I like being busy, or whether I'm like that because of the swimming.

at swimming lessons when I was five years old

School days

I started off going to a private primary school, but didn't like it much. The lessons all went a bit too fast for me and I found it really hard to keep up. Nothing had time to sink in before we moved on to the next thing, so at the end of infant school I moved to another school. It was much better at the new school and I enjoyed most subjects, especially P.E. and Art, because they're sporty and creative. My least favourite subjects were Maths and English – they just seemed quite boring to me, and I didn't understand them, no matter how hard I worked.

I was always happier when I was doing something active.

Aldridge, in the West Midlands, UK

We moved house at the same time as I moved school, to Aldridge, which is where we live now – in a really nice, old house in a large **cul-de-sac**. Although leaving my friends was quite upsetting at the time, because I'm outgoing and friendly I just made new friends very quickly.

It never takes me long to team up with somebody.

with my friend, Vicki Silk, when we were eight years old

5

I had loads of hobbies when I was younger, as well as swimming, of course. There was dancing, ballet, Brownies and horse-riding. I was pretty busy, which was just the way I liked it! When I was eight, I got my own pony, Blodwyn. Having my own pony was a dream come true and I spent a lot of time up at the stables. She's a Welsh pony, so that's why her name is Welsh. She's a bit small, white, quite fat and really cheeky – but very cool. I had to **loan** her to some old friends in the end because I didn't have the time to look after her anymore because of my training.

6

The stables were big, with lots of horses. Blodwyn was the only pony, but I was able to help out a lot with all the other horses – talk to them and feed them – which was brilliant. I loved it up there and had as much fun just spending time with the horses as actually riding Blodwyn. I used to go to the stables about five times a week, but then I started swimming more seriously. I just felt that's where my talent lay and it had to come first. Blodwyn's what I miss most, because I always enjoyed spending time with her and I feel sorry now because I haven't seen her for ages.

me and my pony, Blodwyn

All about me

I've got **Achondroplasia,** which is sometimes called **dwarfism**. It doesn't affect me in a big way, but there are lots of little things that have an **impact** on the way I live. I've got a lot of stools in the kitchen and bathroom because I find it hard to reach things, and if I go to the supermarket on my own I have to ask strangers to get things down from the shelves for me. It's hard if I want to look at something like a magazine because sometimes I just want to flick through it first, but if I've asked someone to get it down for me it's embarrassing to have to ask them to put it back again. It's silly things like that, which are hard.

I remember staying at my aunt's house when I was younger. It's quite an old place and has the old latch doors. When my cousins shut the doors after them I couldn't get out – well, not easily. I could just about get my fingertips to knock the latch off to open the doors. It's those sorts of things that you take for granted, which you might not normally think about – like not being able to have the shoes that you want and having to have all your clothes altered. My feet are only a size two, and sometimes shop assistants put me into children's shoes – but I don't want flowery babyish shoes, I want teenage-looking shoes in a small size.

I think that, and having to wait for new clothes to be altered, are probably the things that I find most annoying. When I buy new clothes, I want to wear them straight away, so it's very frustrating when they don't fit me as they are.

I'm quite lucky though, because everyone at primary school just saw me for who I was and I don't think they took any notice of my disability really, which is exactly what I wanted. When I went to secondary school, I was given some learning support – a teaching assistant who'd help me. I didn't like it because I felt that it separated me from everyone else. I've always just wanted to be with my friends, a regular member of the class, and the extra help made me feel different. The school was good though because they realised straight away that the support wasn't right for me, so they left me to it. They kept an eye on me and told me to ask for help if I needed it, but otherwise I wasn't given any special treatment. I've always had the just-get-on-with-life approach, and my friends and school have generally been the same. They all just see me as Ellie.

PRO★STAR

9

STEVE

The right swimming club for me

We tried two other swimming clubs before finding the right one. At the first one, the teacher basically just carried me around in the pool all lesson because I couldn't touch the floor and he was frightened to death that I'd drown! He just wanted to wrap me up in cotton wool, so I didn't stick with that one for very long. The second one was at the local school and apparently I sat on the side for six weeks complaining that the water was too cold!

It was almost by chance that we ended up at Boldmere Swimming Club. The lesson I went to there was later in the day and because there were just three of us, we got the coach's full attention. At the beginning, I didn't like putting my head back in the water, which meant I wouldn't go on my back at all. So that was the first thing I had to work on. There were loads of little steps in the pool, so the coach would get me to lie on the steps with my head back and get used to having it in the water. Once I could do that, I wasn't worried about it anymore and could then swim on my back, no problem.

My sister swam at the same club. I think she enjoyed it, but unlike me she hasn't got a competitive side to her, she just swam to keep fit. Then, when I started catching her up, I think she just thought, *that's it*, and quit.

Swimming lessons to swimming sessions

I started off learning to swim once a week. Then, when I was about seven and a half, I was invited into the squad. This involved training sessions rather than lessons, so I started to swim twice a week. It was still easy enough fitting in the swimming, because it was just something I did after school. Plus, at primary school I didn't have a lot of homework, so I just saw it as another place to make friends and have fun. I've always liked having separate school friends and swimming friends because it means that there are always so many people to do things with and I do different things with different friends. When I'm with my school friends I don't talk about swimming at all, it's more Justin Bieber and stuff like that!

Getting into the squad came at just the right time because I was ready to go up to the next level and I'd been waiting, wanting to be chosen. During selection, they look for a combination of speed and **technique**, and a general feel for the water. Coaches can apparently see even before you swim whether or not you've got a feel for the water. Back then, my best strokes were **butterfly** and **breaststroke** and those are what I got selected for, but it's funny because those two are now my worst strokes. Butterfly's really hard, I hate it. I much prefer front crawl now – that's probably my favourite.

When I joined the squad, my swimming became much more focused.

Because I was swimming with able-bodied people – there weren't any other disabled people in the squad – I had to work harder to keep up with them. I think that's how I got better quicker. Everyone just treated me like a normal person. Ashley, my coach, never made any exceptions because of my disability, which was good for me.

Six to nine months down the road, Ashley told me that if I wanted to be really good, I'd need to go to sessions three times a week rather than just twice. So that's what I did, and by the time I was ten I was up to about four or five sessions a week.

I must have been getting pretty good, but to be honest, I never thought that much about it. For me it was all about having fun. I liked going to so many sessions a week because I made much closer friendships than I would have done at the once-a-week type of clubs. The changing rooms after the session were always the best bit. We'd spend ages getting changed and there was always lots of laughing and messing around!

Competition time

I'd been going to dwarf athletics for a while. They have Annual Games for all sorts of sports: **boccia**, swimming, cycling, badminton – every sport you can think of, and we used to go every year from when I was very young. I'd always have a go at everything, so I was used to competing in different sports, but against other dwarfs. Then, when I was about eight, I got selected to swim in a **gala** for my club and that was really good because I got to compete against, rather than just train with, able-bodied swimmers.

I didn't win – in fact I came last – but it didn't matter because the fact that I was selected at all was amazing enough and I had such a good time just being with all my friends. It lasted about three hours, but I wanted it to go on longer. I was more excited than nervous to be honest, because I hadn't done this before. It was a new thing for me and that somehow set aside my nerves. During a gala, you might do one race or three or four races as well as **relays**, it just depends on what you're selected for. It's really cool because all your friends are there and it's a team thing – you're cheering each other on.

Star talent

Going to galas and competitions got me noticed and it was at one of these events that I got selected for World Class Talent. It's a programme, which runs across lots of sports, for able-bodied as well as disabled athletes. It finds new, young, talented athletes and helps them to succeed, giving them every chance of becoming professional athletes and making it on to the **podium** at huge sporting events like the Olympics or Paralympics. You get to go away for weekends and to training camps, which are brilliant fun and a great opportunity.

I was the youngest athlete on the programme, but for the first time I got a real sense of how good I was. Because I'd been swimming with able-bodied swimmers for so long, who were twice my size, I didn't realise how much talent I had because I hardly ever won any actual races. But suddenly I could see how well I was doing – the programme publishes your times and I could see in black and white that I was doing the times of an 18-year-old disabled swimmer. It gave me a better understanding of the concept of disability **classification**, times and world records and I realised what I was achieving

Having watched the Athens Paralympics, I started to wonder whether I had a chance of competing at the London Paralympics in 2012. I didn't think I had a chance at the Beijing Paralympics because I was too young. I was asked about going to the Beijing Paralympics in an interview after winning a local BBC Junior Sports award and I said it would be amazing to go, but as I was still only in Year Six, I'd probably be too young. I had no idea what was going to happen and just what a surprise Beijing would turn out to be.

Classification goes from S1 through to S10. S1 is the most severe disability and S10 is almost able-bodied; the "S" stands for Swimming. So in athletics, it's F1 to F10 and the "F" stands for Field, or T1 to T10, and the "T" stands for Track.

Christopher Tronco Sanchez is an S3 classification.

Sometimes you'll look at an S10 and you won't be able to see their disability because it's so slight – they might just have a finger missing. Then at the other end of the scale, an S1 might only be able to swim with one arm, for example. There's an S1

Ludivine Loiseau is an S6 classification.

who can only rock his head – that's how he moves. I don't know how he learnt to swim, but watching him is magical.

My classification is S6, which is about halfway and based on my height. I'm 125 centimetres tall now and if I grow above 130 centimetres I'll go up to an S7, but I'm not likely to grow much more so I don't think my classification will change.

There's a variety of disabilities in my classification; other people with dwarfism, people with **cerebral palsy** on half their side, people with missing legs – it's really about how much power you've got in the water. Every S6, for example, has a similar ability; we're all equal in power, but we could all have totally different disabilities.

What makes it confusing is when you swim against other classifications, so, for example, an S6 against an S7 or an S10. When this happens in races, it's really your time that matters. You get points for your time based on your individual classification's world record for that event, so an S6 would get more points than an S10 if they swam the same time, and the one with the most points wins. It means that the S10 would have to swim faster than the S6 to get as many points.

23

Competing with the stars

I can still remember walking into my first disability gala and seeing so many different types of disabilities, it really surprised me. When I went to warm up there were legs lying at the poolside, because if you had a **prosthetic limb**, you had to take it off to get into the pool. You'd be swimming along and there'd be loads of legs at the side, which was very weird. But that was the only thing that really fazed me and I got used to it pretty quickly.

I also remember being quite shocked, and star-struck, by the sorts of competitors who were there, people who'd competed at the Athens Paralympics, real heroes of mine, like Nyree Lewis, who'd won gold. Nyree's the same classification as me and I've always admired her and what she's achieved. I couldn't believe she was at the same event and in the same pool as me! So, at my first disability gala I was swimming against those who'd swum at the Athens Paralympics.

Nyree Lewis

with the medals I won at the Junior Championships

I did well, considering the competition, but didn't actually win anything. Then a few months after that, I went to my first British Junior Championships. I was ten and in the under-14s category and I won all my races and the trophy for the best performance at the Championships.

It was such a triumph and winning felt amazing. Suddenly my competitive nature kicked in and I just wanted to win all the time! After that I became quite **clinical** about the process. I used to get the programme before an event and look at who I was up against, highlighting the names of those who were getting close to my time so I could see who I needed to beat. My parents used to call it my hit list! But that determination was definitely there by then.

My first World Championships

When I was almost 12 I got selected for the World Championships in Durban, South Africa, to compete against people in my own disability classification. The trials were a few months before and I qualified and made the finals. But, because I was still only 11, it was 50/50 if I'd go because you can't compete internationally until you're 12. I only turned 12 two weeks before the competition, which would have made me the youngest Brit competing. So even though I'd made the time, I didn't think they'd want someone that young on the team.

In order to qualify you're given a competition time that you have to hit for each race. So, for example, as an S6 under-18 girl, I had to swim the 400-metre race in six minutes and 18 seconds, and if I succeeded I'd be considered for selection. Then they publish the team, so you don't actually know until then if you've made it.

My events were the 400-metre **freestyle**, the 100-metre freestyle, the 50-metre freestyle, and the 200-metre IM – Individual Medley. Freestyle means that you can swim any stroke you like, which is usually front crawl because that's the fastest.

IM means you swim a bit of all four strokes, one after
the other, always in the same order: butterfly, backstroke,
breaststroke and freestyle. Luckily I only had to hit
the qualifying time for one of those races. I knew during
the competition that I'd hit the time, but I didn't find out
until later that I'd been selected for the team.

I was away at a camp for kids when my parents got the letter.
I rang home when the camp told me that my parents had
some news. I was really nervous before I found out, because
I didn't think I'd made it. I didn't want to feel let down if I
hadn't, so I kept telling myself that I wouldn't be selected,
that way I might not feel so disappointed if I wasn't.

When I found out that I'd made it, it was even better and more exciting. I was so happy and proud of myself. I was going away to South Africa for a month and I just wanted to tell everybody, just ring up and tell them all. I was over the moon.

The competition itself only lasted for eight or nine days but because South Africa is so hot, we had to go out for much longer to get used to the environment. Although my parents came for the competition itself, I didn't see them much – they weren't even allowed in the hotel and I spent all my time with the team.

Durban, South Africa

We only met up once, for an hour or so on a non-race day, but actually I didn't want to be rushing off to see my parents all the time, because I really wanted to be with the team as much as possible. Also, I was very **conscious** of being the youngest in the team – the next youngest was three years older than me – and I didn't want to be seen as a baby. Anyway, the team members really looked after each other, so it was nice being with them. Luckily, because I'd been away so much on camps and activity weekends, I didn't miss home or my family much at all and just had a great time, soaking up the atmosphere.

We spent the time before the competition training – and, if I'm honest, trying to get a tan! I loved South Africa. It was so nice and hot and we'd drive to the swimming pool every day and see lizards, snakes and monkeys on the road. It was really sunny and the training was all outdoors. The routine was a bit easier than what we'd been doing at home; we tended to cover less distance but trained at a higher **intensity**, perfecting individual skills. Although I was really nervous in the build-up to the competition, I enjoyed the whole experience massively.

Because there were no expectations on me and I didn't think I was actually going to win anything, I just went there to have fun. It was an experience, a new thing for me. What I didn't know at the time, but found out afterwards, was that there were about five or six of us under 16-year-olds who'd been taken there just to give us a taste of an international competition, because they thought we had a chance of qualifying for the Beijing Paralympics. So we were only really meant to be there to get a taste of the competition itself, but I actually did OK and came fifth in some of my races. I made a few finals, but I swam my personal bests in everything, which was pretty good.

A new club, a new life

When I came back to the UK, I knew I needed something to happen – a change in my coaching to get me to the next stage. I was starting to find it frustrating at the club because it was getting harder and harder to keep up with my friends who were the same age as me. As they were growing and the size difference between us got bigger, it got tougher and tougher. They'd go up to the next level before me and I'd get stuck with younger and younger children, and I found that really hard. So, I sat down with my parents and together we talked for ages about my options and came up with loads of ideas.

We thought that I could board at Kelly College, which is a sports college, or possibly move to Swansea where I could be trained by a coach who specialised in my classification – S6. We'd already linked up with Billy, the coach in Swansea, and got on really well with him, so I decided to go with that option and move to Swansea.

It was a big move, but a good one. I'm so happy that we did it because I don't think I'd have gone to Beijing if we hadn't. I needed more than my old club could give me. They couldn't offer me enough pool time, the lanes were **chock-a-block** with children and I couldn't get that focus. I just wasn't happy with it anymore.

34

with Billy Pye, my new coach

We started going to Swansea in the school holidays for the first **intensified** training and I connected with Billy really well. Then, at the end of Year Seven, Mum and I moved there – just in the week – we'd go home every weekend to my dad and siblings, and that's what we're still doing. We drive down to Swansea on a Sunday night, I train and go to school there right through to Saturday. Then my mum picks me up from the pool at 9 o'clock on Saturday morning after training and we head straight back home again. We're used to it now and don't think about it, but at the beginning it was really hard because I had to leave my old friends, my old club and my dad. School was especially hard to start with because everyone had already made friends, but I settled in quickly and it's fine now. It's actually nice that I have my friends in Swansea and then I go home and have my old school friends and swimming friends there – and anyway, I knew straight away that it was the best thing for my swimming, so that made it easier.

the Severn Bridge – the link between Wales and England

A strict schedule

I train four mornings a week from six until half-past seven, and then again after school from half-past three to half-past five, then on a Saturday morning from seven to nine. At the new club we're more focused on competitions, working on skills, and there's more one-to-one tuition – it's a lot more professional and **prescribed**. All ten of us in my group are disabled and coached by Billy, but there are also able-bodied swimmers in other groups with their coaches and we're all in the pool at the same time. It's better than at the old club where one coach would have a group of maybe 30 children. Plus it's got a 50-metre pool, rather than a little squashed one. Sometimes I go back and train at the old club at the weekend and I think, how did I cope with this?

It's got a lot harder fitting in both school and swimming. I have to be very **disciplined** and stick to a strict routine, which I don't really mind because I'm a very organised person. I'm also pretty determined, which you have to be if you want to be the best. I know what I want and am very single-minded about it – training 18 hours a week and being completely focused. Before I go to bed at night, all my bags for school and for swimming are packed for the next day.

But despite the crazy schedule, school's always been important to me, and I don't plan to give up on it just yet. I've already chosen my **A-level** subjects: History, Citizenship and World Development. I really wanted to take Food Technology at A-level too, partly because I got an A* last year, and I'm not an A* person, but I don't think 2012 is the right time for me to tackle too much, not with the London Paralympics as well. I might pick it up again at a later date, but for the time being, I'm trying to keep as much pressure off myself as possible.

It's even harder because I'm in the middle of exams. I'm actually going to have to sit some of my exams out in Majorca because I'll be on a training camp for the European Championships!

My competitions often overlap with schoolwork and it's got harder and harder to juggle the two parts of my life. Once, while I was away swimming, I missed some really important exam preparation work that the rest of the class had to do, which meant playing catch-up when I got back. So, I would get up at half-past five to go swimming, go straight from swimming to school and then spend lunchtime and break doing the work I'd missed. After school, I'd be back in the pool, get home at six o'clock at night and then have to revise for exams. It was a long day without a proper break, but you just have to grit your teeth and get on with it.

because the week's always so **hectic**, I try to relax at weekends. Last Saturday I went to see Justin Bieber in concert. It was amazing. I have a list of the top five things that I've done in my life so far and his concert's up there in my top five. It was a brilliant experience – we were all dancing and singing; it was so good. I love going home at weekends and always look forward to Saturdays and getting back.

Justin Bieber in concert

41

The Beijing Paralympics

I was selected for the Beijing Paralympics when I was 13.
The process was the same as the World Championships –
I hit the time in my 400-metre freestyle, and actually beat
Nyree who was World Champion at the time. I got the
world record as well.

It all came at once and I was so proud of myself. I remember going out to a restaurant with the team that evening and I was so happy I couldn't stop smiling; I was over the moon. Qualifying, getting the world record and beating Nyree – I achieved all three things at once. I was so excited.

Once I'd won the race I was pretty sure I'd be selected for the team, but I had to wait for the letter and for it to be announced on the internet. As with the World Championships, if I went, I'd be the youngest Brit in the team and the youngest British athlete at the entire Games. When I found out, I couldn't believe I was going to Beijing and the Paralympic Games. That's when training got really focused. The coaches spent a lot more time looking carefully at all the little things like skills, starts, turns – everything had to be perfect.

They looked at my lifestyle, nutrition and everything to make sure I was at my best. It was quite a tough regime, but well worth it.

practising my starts, ready for Beijing

the Beijing Paralympic Village

We went to a training camp outside Beijing for two weeks
before the competition to get used to the environment.
Then we went to Beijing for two weeks and into
the Paralympic village, which was so good. Being with
the different teams from all over the world was amazing.
I shared an apartment with six others in a block
of flats for British athletes; it was just brilliant.
I got to see a bit of the city too, some
of the Great Wall of China and
a silk market, but I'd love
to go back and explore more.

I always fiddle with my goggles before a race.

The 200-metre IM was on the first day, which is one of the races I was hoping to get a medal in, but I didn't in the end – I think because I was so nervous. When I'm standing on the blocks before a race, I'm quite fidgety. I'm very aware of my goggles – I don't want them to leak so I'm always touching them and my hat. I'm also thinking about the race. It sounds weird, but I think about whether it's the 100-metre freestyle, or the 400-metre freestyle, I think about how many lengths it is, what stroke it is, how I'm going to swim it; that's all going through my head. The nerves got the better of me on that first day. I just felt that I couldn't do it, so didn't do as well as I'd hoped. But I think missing out on that is what **spurred** me on to go for it in my 100-metre freestyle race the next day, and I qualified second going into the final.

I just thought I could get a medal, so I went for it, which paid off because I came first! I was on such a high, I don't really remember much about the swimming, just that the others were very close to me. We were all in a line, and I thought to myself that I could do it if I just pushed myself a tiny bit harder. When you watch the recording of the race back, you can see that when I actually hit the wall I didn't know I'd won because the race was so close. I'm looking at the scoreboard and you can see the moment when it **registers** because I just started to shake. It was so emotional because it was my dream and I'd tried so hard, I was just so happy with myself; that's why I cried, because I was so happy.

crying with happiness at my 100-metre win

racing in the 400-metre freestyle

The 400-metre race was a few days afterwards, so I had time to get my feet back on the ground and focus, which was good because it was my key event. I was going in as the world record holder, and I'd qualified first in the heats, but even so, I was very nervous. Because I'd won the gold in the 100-metre freestyle race, which I wasn't even supposed to get a medal in, it meant that there was a lot of pressure on me to do well in the 400-metre. It was head to head between me and another swimmer. She was quite fast, but I was beating her in the turns – she didn't get a push off because she's paralysed in the legs. So she was going faster than me, but then at the turn I was coming out in front. It kept going on like that for six lengths.

Then on the last 100 metres, I knew I was going to have to put my head down and go for it. As soon as I touched the wall I knew I'd won. I'd gone in, tried my best, swum really well and got the world record and gold medal. Because the 100-metre race had been such a whirlwind, I took in the win of the 400-metre race much more; I really wanted to **savour** and remember it.

Winning in the 400-metre final was so exciting.

Standing on the podium in front of 17,000 people cheering for me was just amazing; there are no words that can describe it. I was on such a high, knowing that for that moment I was the best in the world.

Once the competition had ended, we all went to the McDonald's in the athletes' village to celebrate. We'd decided before the start of the competition to go there because we'd been on such a strict diet and we just wanted to go and have lots of burgers!

Until then I'd been on a good, healthy, balanced diet with lots of **carbohydrates** for energy, protein and a lot of vegetables and fruit. Generally, swimmers can eat as much as they like because of all the hours of training they do, but because I'm small I have to watch my weight. So McDonald's was a real treat. I didn't get to see any other events at the Games because I had to keep myself focused. We were supporting the team, so we were always at the pool, which meant we didn't really have much time to go and see any other sports. It's a shame because there are lots of other sports, apart from swimming, that I like watching. Wheelchair rugby's one of my favourites – the players are so fierce and it's very cool.

wheelchair rugby

A big come-down

Coming home after the Paralympics was hard. I felt like I had nothing to look forward to or aim towards and so I got quite low; I think partly because I'd been on a high for such a long time. You just come back to earth with a bump and everything feels really boring. Having said that, the first two or three weeks back home were pretty mad because of all the media interest. It was weird because I wasn't used to it. Walking down the street and getting recognised a lot was very strange. I'm used to it now and actually quite enjoy it, but back then it really freaked me out.

One of the most difficult things to deal with was actually an event that my school had organised. They'd sent a **limo** to pick me up and take me to school in the morning.

in the school playground with my Olympic gold medals

There were a lot of media, as well as my whole year group and the new Year Sevens, whom I didn't even know, waiting at the gates. The rest of the school was in the courtyard at the back, and I had to give a talk in front of everyone. I was so embarrassed. I just wanted school to be normal straight away, because there I'm just a normal person with other normal people and all the hype and attention in that environment felt weird.

When I was nominated for the BBC Young Sports Personality of the Year later that year, I was mainly excited to get the chance to go to the event, and just be there with all the sporting legends and top athletes like Bobby Robson and Michael Johnson. I didn't think I'd actually win, especially as I was up against the diver Tom Daley and tennis-star Laura Robson. The organisers could see how nervous I was, so they tried to get me to practise going up on to the stage and saying a few words, but I didn't even want to do that. And because I didn't think I'd win, I didn't think I'd need to practise. I was so sure that Tom was going to get it that I couldn't believe it when I heard my name; it was such a massive surprise. Going up to collect the award was incredibly nerve-wracking, but the footballer Theo Walcott and boxer Ricky Hatton presented it to me, so seeing them was cool. I didn't know what to say because I hadn't prepared anything, so I just thanked everyone and went back to my seat as quickly as I could!

with the diver, Tom Daley

I was so nervous when I collected my award, but so proud to have won.

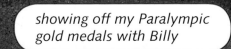

showing off my Paralympic gold medals with Billy

I've grown and developed a lot as an athlete since Beijing. Having won four gold medals at the European Championships and four gold medals at the World Championships, I am now World Champion at four events, and I have three world records. But the Paralympics will always be my best achievement – a Paralympic gold medal is the best medal to have.

I feel a lot more pressure on me now that wasn't there before. Going into Beijing, not many people had really heard of me. But now it's a different story – there's lots of expectation because the next Games are at home and I'm the Paralympic and World Champion. I'm really feeling that, and hoping I live up to it all. At Beijing I just wanted to beat my fellow competitors, but now they've got their eyes on me and I'm the one to beat! But I always tell myself when I go into a competition that I can only swim my best, so that's what I've always tried to do.

I do, however, always have a target that I'm aiming for, whether it's a time I want to achieve, a record I want to beat, or a medal I want to get, so that keeps me focused. At the end of every year, I meet with my coach and think about my targets for the year ahead – key competitions and what I'm aiming to achieve. We work it out together, but sometimes you get surprised, and it's always good to have a surprise.

Meeting the Queen

One of the biggest surprises of all was a letter I received saying that I'd been awarded an **MBE**. I wasn't allowed to tell anybody for a month or two, so only me, my mum and my dad knew – which was cool, because we had to keep it as a surprise from my brother and sisters. I didn't really know what it was at first and had actually just put the letter to one side, but my mum read it and she and my dad explained it to me and I realised what a great thing it was to receive.

It was amazing going to see the Queen. I got made up on a TV programme beforehand and wore high heels for the first time. The shoes were lovely, which was good because it's so hard to find nice shoes, so I was pleased. The producers of the TV programme had bought a selection of outfits for me to choose from, and I got to keep them all, which meant a lot of cool, new clothes, and then they had a stylist do my hair beautifully. I was terrified that I'd somehow mess up the routine that you have to go through, but they make you practise before you do it for real so that there are no mistakes. You always have to face towards the Queen, curtsey, then when she offers you her hand that means you're finished, and you have to walk away backwards so that you don't turn your back on her.

I felt so proud to be given an MBE by the Queen.

I'd decided to bring a pair of substitute flat shoes in my bag, because I'm not used to wearing heels and I thought the worst thing I could do was end up flat on my face in front of the Queen. So when I went from the rehearsal room into the queue for the real thing, I quickly slipped into my flats! Then I put my heels back on for all the photographs afterwards. Billy, my coach, was awarded an MBE on the same day, so it was good to do it with him, and we had such a good time laughing together.

Actually, the Queen was really nice. I thought she'd be a bit posh, but she was lovely, I could've had a full conversation with her. She asked me loads of questions about my favourite stroke and what I hoped to do in the future and congratulated me on what I'd achieved so far. I was amazed how much she knew about each of us, and about my swimming and the medals I've won.

Billy and me with our MBEs

meeting a beefeater

Out in the courtyard afterwards we had great fun, surrounded by **beefeaters**, royal horses, photographers and press. The whole thing was just amazing. Afterwards I went out for a meal with my family, which was a lovely treat.

I think what was amazing about winning gold medals at Beijing were the things I got to do and the opportunities it gave me. I got to go on the Olympic parade, there were TV shows like Blue Peter and Family Fortunes, I met the Queen and got an MBE – all of those good things because of my gold medals and doing what I love.

with Rebecca Adlington and Matt Walker, who also won gold medals in the Olympics

on Family Fortunes

For me, going on Family Fortunes was one of the best things
I've done, because my whole family got to do it with me. It was
really funny and we had a good laugh, but unfortunately we
lost, which didn't go down well with such a competitive family!
Blue Peter was good as well because I used to watch it when I
was younger and to be on it felt pretty special. I got a gold
Blue Peter badge, which I've always wanted. It was almost as
good as a Paralympic gold medal … but not quite!

he difficulty with being famous is thinking that people might be watching you all the time, so you've got to be on your best behaviour. I don't always want to be noticed; sometimes I like to keep myself to myself and that's much harder now. I'm not even that famous. If I was, like some of the pop stars, I don't know how I'd cope. People are really nice and want to congratulate me, but sometimes they call me the "little swimmer", which makes me laugh because it makes me sound like a kid and I'm not. It's funny when you walk past someone in the street and you can hear them talking about you, saying, 'That's the swimmer, that's the swimmer," and I just think, 'Yes, that's me."

I'm getting used to the things that come with fame, like talking on TV.

on the red carpet at the
*Sports Personality of
the Year Awards in 2009*

The Paralympics, 2012

I'm still focused on school, despite where my swimming's taken me. I know that I need to have good exam results to have a good **career** when I'm older. I hope to go to many more Paralympic Games and swim for a long time, but I'm not likely to be swimming professionally in my 30s.

After my swimming career, there are a lot of things I want to do. I'd love to work in the media or maybe as a chef – a **patisserie** person specialising in desserts. I love cooking and baking. I cook for my mum every Thursday night, because I don't train on Thursday afternoons, but my favourite things to cook are muffins and cakes; I do quite a good carrot cake.

After my exams, the big focus is the London
Paralympics. I'll just go out there and swim my
best, qualify first and hopefully regain my titles
and maybe even get a few more. There isn't
one race that I want to do best in, I just hope
to do well in them all. In order to do that, I
need to continue training hard, even when I
don't feel like it. There are times when I just
can't be bothered, if I'm tired or feeling a bit
under the weather, but I always know that I
need to go. I won't get any of the rewards of
swimming unless I train. I've got a lot out of
it over the years – the opportunity to travel the
world, make brilliant friends and have a lot of fun.
There are things that have made it hard and
I've had to give up a lot. I'd prefer to live with
the whole family and be able to go out with
my friends on weeknights, but it's well worth it.

Tanni Grey-Thompson

I never thought I'd have gone through all this by the time I was 16. I thought that it would have happened a lot later, but it's good to have had an early start because it means that I've still got time to achieve a lot more. I'd like to be as big as **Tanni Grey-Thompson**, win more medals and take the recognition of disability sport a lot further. I want to get people out there to know that if they've got a disability, they can still do whatever they want.

Being small has never held me back – I've always felt that I could do anything I wanted. At primary school, I played the giant in the school play one Christmas because when they auditioned for it, that was the part I wanted. My parents have always made me believe that I'm six feet tall, that I can make anything possible and nothing should stop me following my dreams. I think that applies to any disability.

I'm not anything special, just good at what I do. Everybody's good at something, whether they're disabled or able-bodied – it doesn't make a difference, we're all human beings and no one's better than anybody else – we're just better at different things.

Glossary

A-level	an exam in a Secondary School subject that is used as a qualification to enter university
Achondroplasia	a condition some people are born with that affects the growth of their long bones, so they have very short arms and legs
beefeaters	members of the British royal family's guard; they also guard the Tower of London
boccia	a lesser-known Paralympic sport, involving throwing wooden balls on a long, narrow court to get them as close as possible to a target ball
breaststroke	a swimming stroke, swum face down in water on the chest, with arms and legs moving like a frog
butterfly	a swimming stroke that involves moving both arms over the shoulders at the same time, with legs together and kicking at the same time
carbohydrates	starches and sugars found in foods such as bread, cereals, sweets and fruits – used to provide energy
career	an occupation that a person does for a long period of time with the chance to progress
cerebral palsy	a condition that is usually caused by brain damage before or at birth. It affects a person's muscles and can lead to poor co-ordination

chock-a-block	very full of people or things
classification	a class or group into which something is put
clinical	without feeling, and very efficient
conscious	aware of environment or surroundings
cul-de-sac	a road that is closed at one end
dwarfism	a condition affecting a person's growth causing them to be unusually short. Achondroplasia causes about 70% of cases of dwarfism
disciplined	focused on doing what needs to be done, working or behaving in a controlled way
gala	a special sports event, usually a swimming competition
hectic	full of non-stop activity
impact	making an effect or impression
intensified	became more intense or stronger
intensity	great concentration, force or power
limo	short for "limousine" – a luxurious car that is usually driven by a chauffeur driver
loan	lend, allow someone to borrow
MBE	stands for the Member of the Order of the British Empire which is an honour from the Queen

patisserie	a type of French or Belgian bakery that sells mostly pastries and sweets
podium	a raised platform that winners stand on to receive their medal
prescribed	set down as rules or a guide
prosthetic limb	an artificial leg or arm that replaces a missing one
registers	having an effect and making an impression
relays	races between two or more teams. Each team member only participates in part of the race
savour	to enjoy something for as long as possible
siblings	brothers and/or sisters
spurred	being driven to get something done
Tanni Grey-Thompson	one of the most successful disabled athletes in the UK, she has won 11 gold medals in various Paralympic Games
technique	the way of doing a particular task

Index

My route to success

Age 8:
I swam in a gala at my club with able-bodied swimmers.

Age 10:
I was selected for World Class Talent. I realised I was doing the times of an 18-year old disabled swimmer.

Age 5:
I started swimming at Boldmere Swimming Club.

Age 13:
I won the 100-metre race at the Paralympics, Beijing.

Age 13:
I won the 400-metre race at the Paralympics, Beijing.

Age 10:
I competed in my first disability gala.

Age 10:
I swam in my first British Junior Championships and won all my races.

Age 13:
I qualified for the Beijing Paralympics and gained a world record.

Age 12:
I competed in my first World Championships and swam my personal bests.

Age 12:
I moved to Swansea to train with Billy Pye.

⠿ Ideas for reading ⠿

Written by Clare Dowdall BA(Ed), MA(Ed)
Lecturer and Primary Literacy Consultant

Learning objectives: understand underlying themes, causes and points of view; sustain engagement with longer texts using different techniques to make the text come alive; use the techniques of dialogic talk to explore ideas, topics or issues; integrate words, images and sounds imaginatively for different purposes

Curriculum links: Citizenship: Children's rights – human rights; P.E.: Swimming activities and water safety

Interest words: Achondroplasia, technique, disability, podium, Paralympics, classification, cerebral palsy, prosthetic limb, clinical

Resources: whiteboard, internet

Getting started

This book can be read over two or more reading sessions.

- Ask children if they have heard of Ellie Simmonds and what they know about her, e.g. she is a British Swimming Champion.

- Discuss what an autobiography is, and how this book will differ from a biography. Revise the features that are likely to be found in an autobiography, e.g. written mainly in chronological order and in the first person.

- Explain that Ellie Simmonds participates in the Paralympic Games, and brainstorm on the whiteboard any questions children have about Paralympic swimming.

Reading and responding

- Ask children to read from pp2–9, about Ellie's childhood. Discuss what can be deduced about Ellie's family circumstances, e.g. she had a happy early life.

- Discuss why Ellie doesn't introduce her disability until pp8–9. What does this tell the reader about Ellie, e.g. that she doesn't think it is the most important thing about her.

- Ask children to read to the end of the book, noting how Ellie's training schedule and commitment have developed as she's become older.